A Harvest of
Pumpkins and Squash

A Harvest of Pumpkins and Squash: Seasonal Recipes

BY LOU SEIBERT PAPPAS

PHOTOGRAPHS BY MAREN CARUSO

CHRONICLE BOOKS

SAN FRANCISCO

Acknowledgments

It was a joy once again to work with project manager Laurel Leigh, and many thanks to my Gamble Garden friends and testers: Garner Kelly, Caroline Zlotnick, Cecele Quaintance, Kelly Kruse, Colette Rudd, and Dee Gibson.

Text copyright © 2007 by Lou Seibert Pappas.
Photographs copyright © 2007 by Maren Caruso.

ISBN-10: 0-8118-6092-2
ISBN-13: 978-0-8118-6092-5

Manufactured in China.

Designed by Gretchen Scoble
Food Stylist: Kim Konecny
Prop Stylist: Julia Scahill
Digital Assistant: Scott Mansfield

The publisher wishes to thank Williams-Sonoma for providing serving ware, utensils, and other accoutrements used for several of the photos in this book.

10 9 8 7 6 5 4 3 2 1

Chronicle Books LLC
680 Second Street
San Francisco, California 94107

www.chroniclebooks.com

King Arthur is a registered trademark of King Arthur Flour.

Contents

Introduction

In its multitude of forms, squash perennially wins top honors as a versatile, delicious vegetable—as well as a year-round staple. Both winter and summer squash varieties enhance a wealth of savory and sweet dishes. And in spite of its sometimes humble or even homely reputation, squash can be impressive, glamorous, and even fun: beautiful orange butternut squash cut into half-moons and roasted; perfect halves of acorn squash, with the dark green skin striking against the pale yellow flesh, drizzled with caramel; the chayote, hailing from southern climes, used for edible containers for a spicy Middle Eastern lamb stew; long, thin, elegant slices of summer squash making a bed for broiled fish; spaghetti squash baked and topped with a classic meat sauce as a nod to its soft, pastalike strands. Pumpkins, the star of so many porch stages in fall, can turn everyday fare into whimsical and dramatic presentations—a pumpkin soup tureen brimming with chicken soup or stuffed mini pumpkins welcomes diners to a table with a big smile.

For breakfast, lunch, dinner, and dessert, pumpkin and squash are rewarding players in dishes from delicate soufflés to inviting, comfort-food bisques. The repertoire of recipes in this book encompasses delectable muffins, pizza, coffeecakes, and yeast breads; hearty main-course soups and some lighter ones for starters; salads and vegetable accompaniments; pasta and polenta; entrées; and of course, the rich and nutty pies, gingery spice cakes, flan, crème brûlée, ice cream, and cookies that proliferate in fall and feature sweetly in our holiday traditions.

For centuries, pumpkins and squash have graced American hearths and homes. In more recent decades, abundant summer squash have been arguably more prominent, more familiar—except for the hallowed pumpkin—in both the marketplace and backyard gardens. But now, as the demand for locally grown produce and sustainable agriculture grows, savvy purveyors are expanding their bounty with heirloom varieties of both summer and winter squash, and our local greengrocers and farmers' markets are flaunting a wealth of eye-catching squash and pumpkins leading up to the holiday season. New varieties in colorful hues and various shapes and sizes are prompting intrigue for more cooking and sampling.

Now is the perfect time to pick up some pumpkins and squash and enjoy their nourishing goodness for dining around the clock.

—*Lou Seibert Pappas*

THE HERITAGE OF SQUASH

All squash are members of the gourd family known as *Cucurbitaceae*. Most squash belong to the genus *Cucurbita*, which subdivides into the tender-skinned summer squash and the hard-skinned winter squash.

Winter squash are allowed to ripen to maturity so their shell hardens to protect the interior. Some, like butternut and kabocha, are still easy to peel; others require a cleaver or even an ax to puncture the rind. Pumpkins in any size belong to the winter squash family. By contrast, summer squash are picked immature while the skin is tender and the flavor delicate and mild.

Winter squash played a major role on the American frontier. Pilgrims adopted the vegetable, replicating the planting and cooking techniques of Native Americans. They even hollowed pumpkins, stuffed them with apples and maple syrup, and baked them in the coals. Our forefathers valued squash as one of their favorite vegetables because of its excellent keeping quality. But while once regarded as a staple in root cellars, kitchens, and on dinner tables across the country, winter squash experienced a slump in popularity over the last several decades as fast food, trendier vegetables, and speedy cooking came into play.

Today, winter squash have come back into the spotlight, rejoining summer squash as beloved vegetables suitable for steaming, roasting, sautéing, and puréeing. Besides having deep flavor, the rich source of nutrients—in particular beta-carotene—is a key to the upswing in popularity for winter squash. Summer squash, nutritional champions in their own right, continue to be cherished in every season for their fresh flavors, speedy cooking, and tastiness in the raw state.

BUYING, STORING, AND COOKING SQUASH

Winter Squash

There is a plethora of winter squash varieties, many of which are now standard features at produce markets. They differ greatly in size, shape, and exterior color, yet all have a sweet yellow or orange flesh. (That colorful flesh reflects the fact that most winter squash are a great source of vitamins and minerals. One of the most prevalent nutrients is beta-carotene, which has powerful antioxidant and anti-inflammatory properties. Winter squash also contain vitamin C, potassium, dietary fiber, omega-3 fatty acids, and various B vitamins.) When selecting, look for squash with dull skins and a heavy feel. Lighter, shinier squash may not be fully ripe.

Winter squash are at their prime from September to February. Excellent keepers, they will stay fresh for up to six months if stored in a dry, dark place. Use as pretty centerpieces before cooking. Once cut, wrap in plastic and refrigerate.

Unlike summer squash, which are good to eat raw, winter squash must be cooked. Cooking tenderizes their fibers and turns them smooth and creamy. Home cooks are discovering how easy it is to microwave, bake, and roast winter squash. (Boiling and steaming tend to introduce more water into the squash and so they are less appealing cooking methods.)

As you cook with winter squash varieties, it is easy to develop favorites. Butternut rates high for all-around versatility in soups, pies, casseroles, and breads, with its rich, deep orange, fine-textured flesh. Kabocha and buttercup are not quite as sweet but are excellent, too. Acorn is a natural for baking and serving in the half-shell. More mild-flavored banana and Hubbard squash are ideal for serving as a side dish. Note, although most winter squash can be used interchangeably in recipes, spaghetti squash is an exception. It is more like a cross between a summer and winter variety; when cooked, the interior separates into pale golden filaments that are moist and tender like zucchini—and yes, like spaghetti!

The best pumpkins for cooking and baking are small to medium pie pumpkins such as Sugar, Sugar Pie, New England Pie, Baby Bear, or Triple Treat. Some of the newer ornamental white varieties, such as Lumina or Fairytale, are good both for decoration and eating. The pantry standby, canned pumpkin purée, is now widely available from many high-quality producers and is a fine choice for many dishes, as well as in a pinch. Winter squash purées are readily available as well.

To prepare winter squash for cooking, first rinse the squash. Cut it in half lengthwise or cut off a topknot if using the shell for a container. A cleaver is a useful tool on very hard rinds if halving; use a very sturdy knife to cut out tops. Scoop out the seeds and fibers and discard (unless you are going to toast the seeds). Cut large squash into serving size pieces.

The easiest method for cooking winter squash is baking it in a conventional oven or cooking it in a microwave oven. Place squash halves cut side down in a parchment paper–lined baking dish and bake at 350° to 375°F until tender when pierced with a knife, 50 minutes to 1 hour. Or, microwave in a covered dish with a tablespoon or two of water for 7 to 10 minutes per pound; let stand a few minutes to finish cooking.

Appliance experts recommend preheating an oven for 30 minutes before baking. This is especially important with newer ovens. It is smart to check your oven with a portable oven thermometer placed in the oven. The recipes in this book include doneness cues plus cooking time ranges.

Roast squash by cutting it into small chunks, tossing it with olive oil and seasonings, and baking it in a parchment-lined dish at 375° to 400°F, stirring occasionally, until lightly browned and tender, 45 minutes to 1 hour, depending on the size of the pieces.

Cooked pumpkin or squash can be puréed in a blender or food processor and used in soups or baked dishes. You can refrigerate a purée for up to 2 days, or freeze in an airtight container for up to 1 month.

Complementary seasonings for winter squash include sweet, fruity, and spicy flavors such as brown sugar, maple syrup, cinnamon, allspice, cloves, nutmeg, crystallized ginger, sage, rosemary, garlic, cumin, coriander, red pepper flakes, curry, as well as sharp cheeses like Gruyère, Parmesan, and Pecorino Romano.

Plan on about 1½ pounds of trimmed winter squash for four persons.

Summer Squash

Select comparatively fragile summer squash carefully for maximum quality of flavor and nutrition. The squash should have bright glossy skins and be free from bruises or mold.

Small to medium summer squash are preferable as larger ones can be seedy, watery, and less flavorful. Pick specimens that are firm and heavy for their size.

Summer squash are at their peak season July through September, though they are available year-round. Refrigerate summer squash unwashed in an unsealed plastic bag in the vegetable section of the refrigerator and use within 3 or 4 days.

Summer squash require little or no cooking. The different varieties can be used interchangeably in cooking. Wash them just before using and do not peel unless specified. Slice, dice, or shred and sauté, steam, or grill them. Or microwave sliced squash, allowing 7 minutes per pound.

Flavors complementary to summer squash include garlic, olive oil, yogurt, Parmesan cheese, goat cheese, pine nuts, walnuts, parsley, basil, thyme, oregano, dill, mint, and lemon.

Allow 4 to 8 ounces of summer squash per person.

Refer to Types of Squash on pages 12–13 for more details and advice for selecting squash.

TYPES OF SQUASH

Winter Squash Varieties

ACORN (DANISH, TABLE QUEEN)
The most familiar winter squash, acorn has dark green skin, often mottled with orange; choose ones with as much green on the rind as possible. The fluted shell yields a yellow-gold interior of mild-flavored flesh. It tends to be a bit bland and is often sweetened with brown sugar or maple syrup. Lower in beta-carotene but higher in calcium than other varieties. Available year-round.

BANANA
A large 3- or 4-foot-long cylinder that is often sold cut in slabs. The hard pinkish rind yields fine-grained pale orange flesh that is mild in flavor. It is fairly easy to peel. Smaller varieties, such as Banana Blue, are reliable for quality.

BUTTERCUP
Round and dark green with a gray-green blossom end. The meat has a sweet, nutlike flavor but may be dry, so look for signs of freshness (see page 9). Typically weighs 3 to 5 pounds.

BUTTERNUT
This buff-colored squash has a long, solid neck and a fat bulge at one end that contains small seeds good for toasting. The thin tan skin belies the rich, dense, deep orange flesh beneath. It has less water and strings than most winter squash, and its vibrant orange color provides a rich source of beta-carotene. One of the best-tasting winter squash, butternut makes a choice purée and is excellent roasted. It is also the easiest to peel. Average weight is 2 to 3 pounds.

CARNIVAL
A recent cross between acorn and Sweet Dumpling, with both horizontal and vertical stripes in bright orange, green, and gold on the pale beige flesh. A neat, small, round size, often 12 ounces to 1 pound, with fibrous flesh.

DELICATA
Yellow, orange, or cream-colored rind with dark green stripes on an elongated shape. The skin is easy to peel. This is one of the quickest-cooking winter squash, yielding a sweet, delicate flavor. Typically weighs ½ pound and up.

GOLD NUGGET
This varietal has a tiny, fluted pumpkin shape and is very firm, with a hard rind. The skin is orange, often with a green stripe around the stem. The sweet, moist meat can be bland if picked immature. Best to microwave or bake it whole due to the hard rind.

HUBBARD (BLUE, BABY BLUE, GOLDEN, GREEN WARTED)
The big Hubbard has slate-colored, orange, tan, or blue-grey thick skin that may be smooth or warty. It is shaped like a child's spinning top. Typically weighs 8 to 12 pounds but some, like the Baby Blue, are small. Often sold by the chunk.

KABOCHA (ALSO CALLED JAPANESE PUMPKIN)
Jade green rind with tender skin and outstandingly rich, deep orange flesh. Available almost all year. Nice compact flattened-round size.

PUMPKINS (SUGAR, SUGAR PIE, NEW ENGLAND PIE, BABY BEAR, TRIPLE TREAT)
For cooking, pick a Sugar or Sugar Pie, New England Pie, Baby Bear, or Triple Treat. White varieties, such as Lumina, are also good for cooking and carving. Eating pumpkins are hard to find after Thanksgiving.

PUMPKINS, LARGE FIELD

Produced commercially for Halloween, these now come in myriad varieties with names such as Baby Bear, Ghost Rider, Happy Jack, Howden Field, and Prizewinner. Yet the jack-o'-lanterns do not have the best flavor for cooking. Best for carving.

PUMPKINS, MINI (JACK BE LITTLE, MUNCHKIN)

Orange and white skin with orange meat mildly sweet. The large seed cavity makes a nice size for stuffing. Can weigh from 4 to 16 ounces.

SPAGHETTI SQUASH

Within the pale yellow, oval-shaped rind, the cooked flesh easily separates into spaghetti-like strands with a mild, nutty flavor. This squash has its own unique character and is not used mashed or puréed like the other winter varieties. Available year-round.

SUGAR LOAF

Related to delicata; cylindrical in shape. The skin is light tan with dark green stripes. Yellow, firm, medium-dry meat with rich, sweet flavor. Sugar Loafs have a large seed cavity ideal for stuffing.

SWAN WHITE

Acorn shaped with pale yellow flesh and delicate, sweet flavor, free of pumpkin taste.

SWEET DUMPLING

Developed in Japan. Green stripes on a cream background that turns orange over yellow as it matures. Pale yellow-orange meat. Typically weighing 1 to 1½ pounds, Sweet Dumplings are a nice size for stuffing.

TURBAN (ALSO CALLED TURK'S TURBAN)

Turbans are fanciful looking, like a clown's hat with multi-striped knobs. With their fibers and lack of flavor, they are ideal for décor rather than baking.

Summer Squash Varieties

CHAYOTE (ALSO CALLED MIRLITON, CHRISTOPHENE, VEGETABLE PEAR, XUXU)

Pear-shaped; light to dark green and slightly rippled, smooth skin. Grown in the tropics of Mexico and Central America, and in Florida. Similar to summer squash but requires longer cooking. Belongs to the genus *Sechium,* a relative of the *Cucurbita* clan (see page 8). Contains one flat edible seed and has a slight cucumber flavor. Typically weighs about ¾ pound.

CROOKNECK AND YELLOW STRAIGHT-NECK

These common summer squash have pale yellow to deep golden skin that is a combination of smooth and bumpy, and flesh that is yellow throughout the interior. Crookneck, with its curved neck, is a forerunner. The yellow straight-neck was developed for easier packing and shipping. This squash has large tender seeds, an excellent flavor, and is available most of the year.

PATTYPAN (ALSO CALLED SCALLOP, CYMLING)

A scalloped edge distinguishes these compact squash shaped like a flattened disk. Pattypan comes with skin in various shades of green and gold. Pale green types become white as they grow larger. Hybrids include the bright yellow Sunburst and the dark green Scallopini, a cross between pattypan and zucchini. The peak season is July through September.

ZUCCHINI (ALSO CALLED ITALIAN SQUASH, COURGETTE)

Long, straight, and cylindrical, with smooth skin in shades of light to dark green and white or very pale green flesh. Gold Rush is a bright yellow hybrid. The small, round, firm Ronde de Nice is a French heirloom zucchini. The standard green-skinned varieties are available year-round.

Delectable muffins, scrumptious coffeecake, wholesome quick loaves,
and comforting pumpkin bread fill the breakfast or teatime table with tantalizing
aromas. A puffy pumpkin pancake, fluffy waffles, and a savory frittata loaded
with fresh herbs offer other delights for breakfast or brunch, and a
beautiful thin-crust two-squash pizza will dazzle on any table.

Breads and Breakfast

Rosemary-Polenta Pumpkin Muffins

Rosemary lends an intriguing savory flavor to these crusty-topped little cakes. Serve them for brunch or a dessert snack any time of day. The polenta provides a subtle crunch throughout. You can also bake the batter in a round pan for a coffeecake. MAKES 20 MUFFINS OR ONE 9-INCH CAKE; SERVES 12

¼ cup minced fresh rosemary

2 teaspoons grated lemon zest

2 cups confectioners' sugar,
    plus 1 teaspoon

1⅔ cups all-purpose flour

½ cup polenta

2 teaspoons baking powder

3 teaspoons ground cinnamon

¾ teaspoon ground allspice

¼ teaspoon salt

4 large eggs

¾ cup olive oil

¾ cup pumpkin purée, canned
    or homemade

2 tablespoons demerara or raw sugar

Preheat the oven to 350°F. Line 20 standard muffin cups with paper liners, or line the bottom of a 9-inch springform pan with parchment paper and butter the sides of the pan.

In a small bowl, combine the rosemary and zest and mash with the 1 teaspoon confectioners' sugar. In a large bowl, stir together the 2 cups confectioners' sugar, the flour, polenta, baking powder, cinnamon, allspice, and salt. Add the eggs and the rosemary mixture. Using an electric mixer set on medium speed, beat until blended. Slowly pour in the oil, beating until smooth. Add the pumpkin and beat until smooth, about 2 minutes longer.

Spoon the batter into the prepared muffin cups, filling each three-fourths full, or spread in the prepared cake pan. Sprinkle with the demerara sugar. Bake until a toothpick inserted into the center comes out clean, 18 to 20 minutes for muffins or 45 to 50 minutes for coffeecake. Transfer to a wire rack and let cool slightly, then turn the muffins out onto the rack or remove the sides of the springform pan, if using. Serve warm or at room temperature. Store in an airtight container at room temperature for up to 2 days, or wrap tightly and freeze for up to 1 month.

Cranberry-Walnut Pumpkin Coffeecake

Fresh cranberries burst with tangy flavor, but dried cranberries are also excellent in this nut-laced quick coffee bread. The batter goes together in short order for a delicious breakfast or brunch flourish or a welcome sweet snack with coffee later in the day. If you want to freeze the cake, just cut it first; the serving pieces will heat almost instantly in a microwave. SERVES 12

1 cup chopped walnuts or pecans

1¼ cups all-purpose flour

⅓ cup white or yellow cornmeal

1 teaspoon baking soda

½ teaspoon salt

1½ teaspoons ground cinnamon

1 teaspoon ground ginger

¼ teaspoon ground cloves

2 large eggs

¾ cup granulated sugar

½ cup firmly packed light brown sugar

⅓ cup canola oil

⅓ cup sour cream

1 cup pumpkin or winter squash purée, canned or homemade

1 cup fresh or dried cranberries

3 tablespoons demerara or raw sugar

Preheat the oven to 350°F. Butter and flour a 9-inch square baking pan.

Spread the walnuts in a small baking pan and bake until lightly toasted, 8 to 10 minutes.

In a medium bowl, whisk together the flour, cornmeal, baking soda, salt, cinnamon, ginger, and cloves. In a large bowl, combine the eggs, granulated sugar, brown sugar, oil, sour cream, and pumpkin and beat with a large whisk or an electric beater until smooth. Add the dry ingredients to the pumpkin mixture and mix just until incorporated. Stir in the cranberries and ⅔ cup of the nuts. Scrape the batter into the prepared pan and smooth the top. Scatter the remaining ⅓ cup nuts on top and sprinkle with the demerara sugar.

Bake until a toothpick inserted into the center comes out clean, 30 to 35 minutes. Transfer to a wire rack and let cool in the pan to room temperature, then cut into 12 rectangles. Store in an airtight container at room temperature for up to 2 days, or wrap tightly and freeze for up to 1 month.

Zucchini—Golden Raisin Quick Bread

Shredded zucchini keeps this quick bread moist. Slice thinly and spread with cream cheese for impressive and satisfying open-face tea sandwiches. It is also an ideal bread to wrap and give as a gift. A new organic white whole-wheat flour on the market tastes milder and bakes lighter than traditional whole wheat; King Arthur makes a readily available version. MAKES ONE 9-BY-5-INCH OR TWO 7-BY-3-INCH LOAVES; SERVES 12

1 medium zucchini (about 8 ounces), finely shredded

⅔ cup canola or olive oil

½ cup granulated sugar

½ cup firmly packed light brown sugar

2 large eggs

¾ cup organic white whole-wheat flour or whole-wheat flour

¾ cup all-purpose flour

1 teaspoon baking powder

½ teaspoon baking soda

½ teaspoon salt

1 teaspoon ground cinnamon

½ teaspoon ground allspice

1 teaspoon vanilla extract

½ cup golden raisins

½ cup roasted sunflower seeds, plus ¼ cup more for sprinkling (optional)

Preheat the oven to 350°F. Butter and flour one 9-by-5-inch loaf pan or two 7-by-3-inch loaf pans.

Turn out the zucchini onto plastic wrap on a work surface and pat dry with paper towels.

In a large bowl, combine the oil, granulated sugar, brown sugar, and eggs and beat until thoroughly blended.

In a medium bowl, stir together the whole-wheat and all-purpose flours, baking powder, baking soda, salt, cinnamon, and allspice. Add the flour mixture to the egg mixture and beat until smooth. Stir in the vanilla, raisins, zucchini, and ½ cup sunflower seeds. Scrape the batter into the prepared pan(s) and smooth the top. Sprinkle with sunflower seeds if desired.

Bake until a toothpick inserted into the center comes out clean, 50 to 60 minutes for the larger pan or about 35 minutes for the two smaller pans. Transfer to a wire rack and let cool in the pan(s) for 10 minutes. Remove from the pan(s) and let cool completely on the rack. Store in an airtight container at room temperature for up to 2 days, or wrap tightly and freeze for up to 1 month.

Orange-Frosted Pumpkin Muffins
with Spooky Faces

A touch of orange marries a simple, silky frosting with the classic spiced-pumpkin flavor of these moist golden muffins. Children will enjoy decorating the frosting with dried fruit and candies to create fun faces for the spooky season, or to make any occasion festive. MAKES 12 MUFFINS

½ cup (1 stick) butter, at room
    temperature

⅔ cup firmly packed light brown
    sugar

¼ cup molasses

1 cup pumpkin or winter squash
    purée, canned or homemade

2 large eggs

2 cups all-purpose flour

1 teaspoon baking soda

1½ teaspoons ground cinnamon

½ teaspoon ground ginger

½ teaspoon salt

¾ cup golden raisins

ORANGE FROSTING:

1 cup confectioners' sugar

2 tablespoons butter, melted

1 tablespoon thawed orange juice
    concentrate

Raisins, dried cranberries or cherries,
chocolate chips, candy corn, and
sprinkles for decorating, or other
tidbits of your choice

Preheat the oven to 400°F. Line 12 standard muffin cups with paper liners.

In a large bowl, combine the butter, brown sugar, and molasses. Using an electric mixer set on medium speed, beat until creamy. Add the pumpkin and eggs and beat until smooth. In another bowl, stir together the flour, baking soda, cinnamon, ginger, and salt. Add the dry ingredients to the pumpkin mixture along with the raisins and mix just until incorporated.

Spoon the batter into the prepared muffin cups, filling each almost to the rim, and smooth the tops. Bake for 15 minutes, or until a toothpick inserted in the center comes out clean. Transfer to a wire rack and let cool slightly, then turn the muffins out and let cool completely in their liners on the rack.

Meanwhile, make the frosting: In a small bowl, beat together the confectioners' sugar, butter, and orange juice concentrate. Spread over the cooled muffins. Decorate with the dried fruit, chocolate chips, candies, and sprinkles as you like, making whimsical faces. Serve at room temperature.

Sautéed Apple—Pumpkin Oven Pancake

*Sautéed apple slices make a delicious cushion for a puffy pumpkin pancake in this intriguing varia-
tion on the classic Dutch Baby. Preheat the baking dish in the oven before adding the fruit and batter
to give the pancake an instant boost. Serve the pancake right away, as it deflates fairly quickly after
it comes out of the oven. Accompany with real maple syrup.* SERVES 4 TO 6

3 tablespoons butter

4 large apples such as Granny Smith,
    Gala, or Golden Delicious, peeled,
    cored, and cut into ⅜-inch slices

4 tablespoons firmly packed light
    brown sugar

1½ teaspoons ground cinnamon

4 large eggs

⅔ cup pumpkin or winter squash
    purée, canned or homemade

⅔ cup whole milk

⅔ cup unbleached all-purpose flour

1 teaspoon vanilla extract

⅛ teaspoon salt

Confectioners' sugar for dusting

Preheat the oven to 425°F.

In a large skillet, melt 2 tablespoons of the butter over
medium-high heat. Add the apples and sauté just until
tender, 5 to 7 minutes. Sprinkle with 2 tablespoons of the
sugar and ½ teaspoon of the cinnamon and stir to coat the
apples. Remove from the heat.

Place a 10- or 11-inch round soufflé or casserole dish in the
oven to heat for 5 minutes. Remove the dish from the oven,
add the remaining 1 tablespoon butter, and tilt the dish to
coat the bottom. Spoon the sautéed apples over the bottom
of the dish.

In a blender, combine the eggs, pumpkin, milk, flour, the
remaining 2 tablespoons sugar and 1 teaspoon cinnamon,
the vanilla, and the salt and blend for a few seconds, just
to incorporate. Scrape down the sides of the jar and blend
again to incorporate.

Pour the batter over the hot apples. Bake until puffed and
golden brown, 20 to 25 minutes. Dust with the confectioners'
sugar and serve immediately.

Pumpkin-Orange Waffles
with Hazelnut—Maple Syrup Butter

Toasted hazelnuts in whipped butter lend a decadent crunch to these golden waffles for a real treat for brunch. The waffles freeze very well, ready to reheat in a toaster or regular oven at 300°F until hot throughout. It is smart to toast and skin a quantity of hazelnuts in advance so they are ready to pop into the sweet butter. MAKES ABOUT EIGHT 7-INCH ROUND WAFFLES; SERVES 8

HAZELNUT–MAPLE SYRUP BUTTER:

⅓ cup hazelnuts

6 tablespoons butter, at room
   temperature

6 tablespoons pure maple syrup

2 cups all-purpose flour

⅓ cup firmly packed light brown
   sugar

2 teaspoons baking powder

½ teaspoon baking soda

1½ teaspoons ground cinnamon

½ teaspoon ground ginger

¼ teaspoon salt

3 large eggs, separated

¾ cup puréed pumpkin or winter
   squash, canned or homemade

1½ cups whole milk

1 cup freshly squeezed orange juice

⅓ cup unsalted butter, melted

To make the Hazelnut–Maple Syrup Butter, preheat the oven to 350°F. Spread the hazelnuts in a baking pan. Bake until lightly toasted, about 10 minutes. Remove from the oven and rub the hazelnuts between paper towels while they are still warm, letting the papery skins fall off. Chop the nuts finely.

In a small bowl, combine the butter and syrup and beat with a wooden spoon until light and fluffy. Stir in the nuts. Scrape into a serving bowl. (Or, heat the butter, syrup, and nuts, stir, and pour into a pitcher.)

Preheat a waffle iron. In a large bowl, whisk together the flour, sugar, baking powder, baking soda, cinnamon, ginger, and salt. In a medium bowl, beat or whisk together the egg yolks, pumpkin, milk, orange juice, and melted butter. In another medium bowl, using an electric mixer set on medium high speed, beat the egg whites until soft, glossy peaks form. Add the pumpkin mixture to the dry ingredients and mix just until combined. Fold in the egg whites.

Spoon or pour about ¾ cup batter onto the hot iron. Close the lid. Cook according to the manufacturer's instructions until the waffle is golden brown, 4 to 5 minutes. Remove with a fork to a warmed plate. Serve at once or keep warm on a baking sheet in a 200°F oven. Repeat with the remaining batter. Pass the Hazelnut–Maple Syrup Butter with the warm waffles.

Roman Squash Duo Pizza

Years ago on a trip to Italy, I discovered crispy, ultrathin disks of platter-sized pizzas studded with different toppings in the casual trattorias in Rome. This pizza makes an addictive entrée, and it can be varied in impromptu fashion since the dough keeps well in the refrigerator for up to 3 days—just wrap the pieces loosely in plastic after dividing (if refrigerated, bring the dough to room temperature before rolling out). MAKES FOUR 10-INCH PIZZAS; SERVES 8

DOUGH:

¾ cup warm (105° to 115°F) water

1 package (2¼ teaspoons) active
    dry yeast

1 teaspoon sugar

2 cups unbleached all-purpose flour
    or bread flour, plus extra for
    kneading

¾ teaspoon salt

1 large egg

1 tablespoon olive oil

TOPPING:

¼ cup olive oil

1 large red onion, chopped

4 small yellow straight- or crookneck
    squash, thinly sliced

4 small zucchini, thinly sliced

8 ounces brown cremini mushrooms
    (about 24), thinly sliced

8 plum (Roma) tomatoes, sliced

8 ounces mozzarella or Monterey Jack
    cheese, thinly sliced

1 cup (8 ounces) freshly grated Pecor-
    ino Romano or Parmesan cheese

¾ cup torn or minced fresh basil

Fresh basil sprigs for garnish

To make the dough, place the warm water in a large bowl and sprinkle in the yeast and sugar. Let stand until dissolved and puffy, about 10 minutes. Beat in 1 cup of the flour, the salt, the egg, and the oil until blended. Gradually add the remaining 1 cup flour, beating with a heavy-duty mixer or by hand until the dough comes together in a ball. Transfer the dough to a lightly floured work surface and knead a few times until no longer sticky, dusting with additional flour if needed.

Form the dough into a ball and place in a lightly oiled bowl. Cover with plastic wrap and let rise until doubled in bulk, about 1 hour. Gently remove the dough from the bowl, place on a lightly floured work surface, and divide into 4 equal pieces.

Preheat the oven to 500°F. If desired, place a pizza stone on the middle rack.

In a very large skillet, heat the oil over medium heat. Add the onion and sauté until soft, about 8 minutes. Push the onion to the side of the pan, add all of the squash, and sauté for 2 minutes. Add the mushrooms and toss and stir until heated through, then stir the onions back in.

continued >

On a lightly floured work surface, roll out a piece of dough into a 10-inch round. Place the dough round on an oiled pizza pan or baking sheet or on a pizza peel generously sprinkled with cornmeal. Spread one-fourth of the vegetables evenly over the round, leaving a ½-inch border around the edge of the dough. Arrange one-fourth of the sliced tomatoes over the vegetables, then cover with one-fourth of the mozzarella slices.

Place the pizza in the oven or onto the preheated stone, if using. Bake until the crust is crisp and browned, 6 to 7 minutes. Sprinkle with ¼ cup of the romano cheese and 3 tablespoons of the torn basil, and garnish with basil sprigs. Repeat to make the remaining 3 pizzas, assembling the next pizza while one is baking. Cut into quarters to serve as a first course or appetizer, or cut in half for a brunch or lunch entrée.

Squash and Tomato Oven Frittata

When the zucchini and other tender, colorful squash are at their bountiful peak in summer, create this easy one-pan egg dish for a brunch or luncheon entrée or appetizer dish. SERVES 6

5 medium summer squash such as zucchini and yellow straight- or crookneck, in any combination (about 1½ pounds total)

1 teaspoon salt

3 tablespoons olive oil

2 shallots or green onions, including tender green tops, chopped

1 clove garlic, minced

2 plum (Roma) tomatoes, seeded (see Note page 37) and diced

6 large eggs

2 tablespoons freshly grated Parmesan or Pecorino Romano cheese

Freshly ground black pepper to taste

1 tablespoon minced fresh oregano or ¾ teaspoon dried oregano

½ cup (2 ounces) shredded Jarlsberg or Gruyère cheese

3 tablespoons minced fresh basil

2 tablespoons minced fresh flat-leaf (Italian) parsley

Trim the squash and slice very thinly, about ¼ inch thick. Transfer to a colander, sprinkle with the salt, and set aside to drain for 15 to 20 minutes; rinse and pat dry.

In a large skillet, heat 1 tablespoon of the oil over medium heat. Add the squash and sauté until crisp-tender, 4 to 5 minutes. Transfer to a plate lined with paper towels to drain. Add 1 teaspoon of the oil to the skillet and sauté the shallots and garlic for 1 minute. Add the tomatoes and cook until heated through; transfer to a plate and set aside.

In a large bowl, whisk the eggs with the Parmesan and pepper. Heat the remaining 5 teaspoons oil in the skillet over medium heat, spread the squash over the pan bottom, and sprinkle with the oregano. Pour in the egg mixture and cook until set, about 5 minutes. Meanwhile, preheat the broiler. Top the frittata with the tomato mixture, Jarlsberg, basil, and parsley. Slip under the broiler just to melt the cheese, about 1 minute.

Cut into wedges and serve warm or at room temperature.

Pumpkin shells big and little make neat containers for midwinter soups.
Kabocha, butternut, and delicata squash enhance autumn salads.
Acorn and other winter squash and pumpkin play a starring role in
comforting, healthy side dishes.

Soups, Salads, and Sides

Butternut Squash—Pear Bisque

I used winter pears from my garden for a subtle fruity sweetness when I developed this delicious version of a golden squash soup. It is superb served with a garnish of shredded extra-sharp Vermont or Canadian Cheddar cheese. Or, scatter over toasted Garlic Sourdough Croutons (page 52) or crispy toasted squash seeds (see page 33). SERVES 6

2 tablespoons butter

1 medium onion, diced

1 medium butternut squash (about 2 pounds), peeled, seeded, and cut into 1-inch chunks

1 large Anjou pear, peeled, halved, cored, and cut into chunks

1 parsnip or carrot, peeled and cut into chunks

1 quart homemade or canned low-sodium chicken broth

1 bay leaf

1 tablespoon honey

½ teaspoon dried thyme

Salt and freshly ground black pepper to taste

½ cup heavy (whipping) cream or whole milk

½ cup shredded extra-sharp Cheddar cheese or Garlic Sourdough Croutons (page 52)

In a large pot, melt the butter over medium heat. Add the onions and sauté until translucent, 8 minutes. Add the squash, pear, and parsnip and sauté for a few minutes longer. Raise the heat to high and add the broth, bay leaf, honey, and thyme. Season lightly with salt. Bring to a boil, reduce the heat to low, and simmer until the squash is very soft, about 15 minutes.

Remove the bay leaf and let the soup cool slightly. Working in 2 or 3 batches, in a blender or food processor fitted with the metal blade, process the soup to a smooth purée. Alternatively, use an immersion blender to purée the soup in the pot. Return the soup to the pot if necessary and stir in the cream. Taste and adjust the seasoning with salt and pepper. Stir over low heat until the soup is hot throughout. Ladle into bowls and garnish with the cheese or croutons. Serve immediately.

Chicken and Vegetable Soup in a Big Pumpkin

For a festive occasion, use a hollowed-out field pumpkin as a serving container for this nourishing chicken and vegetable soup. Let the guests augment their bowlful with a selection of condiments for rich and colorful flavor and contrast. SERVES 6 TO 8

6 skinless chicken thighs

1½ quarts homemade or canned
low-sodium chicken broth

1 medium onion, quartered

1 stalk celery, chopped

½ teaspoon salt

½ teaspoon freshly ground black
pepper

1 medium pumpkin (about 8 pounds)

1 clove garlic, minced

½ teaspoon dried oregano

½ teaspoon ground cumin

Dash of hot pepper sauce

2 cups diced pumpkin, banana squash,
or Hubbard squash (½-inch dice)

2 cups fresh corn kernels (from about
4 ears yellow or white corn)

2 yellow straight- or crookneck
squash, sliced

TOPPINGS:

½ cup toasted pumpkin seeds
(see Note)

½ cup chopped fresh cilantro

1 red bell pepper, halved, seeded,
and diced

½ cup (2 ounces) grated Monterey
Jack cheese

Preheat the oven to 375°F.

In a large saucepan, combine the chicken, broth, onion, celery, salt, and pepper. Cover and bring to a boil over medium-high heat. Reduce the heat to low and simmer for 45 minutes.

While the chicken is cooking, cut off the top of the pumpkin, leaving the sides tall and sturdy but making enough room for easy ladling. Scoop out the seeds and reserve for toasting. Place the pumpkin shell on a baking sheet. Bake for 15 minutes.

Using tongs, transfer the chicken thighs to a plate. When cool enough to handle, remove the meat from the bones and tear it into strips using your fingers or 2 forks. Discard the bones. Skim off the fat from the broth and strain through a fine-mesh sieve into a large bowl. Return the broth to the pot. Add the garlic, oregano, cumin, hot pepper sauce, and diced pumpkin. Bring to a boil, then reduce the heat and simmer for 15 minutes. Add the chicken, corn, and yellow squash and simmer for 5 minutes longer. Pour the hot soup into the hot pumpkin shell. Serve, accompanied with the toppings.

NOTE: To toast pumpkin seeds, separate the seeds from the fibers and rinse them. Place in a bowl with 1 teaspoon soy sauce and 2 teaspoons balsamic vinegar and stir to combine and coat. Let stand for 30 minutes. Preheat the oven to 300°F. Place the seeds on a parchment-lined baking sheet. Bake until lightly browned, about 30 minutes.

Cheese Soup in Little Pumpkin Shells

Individual decorative pumpkins or other small, round winter squash make charming containers for this wine-laced cheese soup. Accompany with crusty rosemary bread and a salad of arugula and mixed greens tossed with red grapes and toasted pecans. SERVES 6

6 mini pumpkins or Carnival, Sweet Dumpling, or acorn squash (¾ to 1 pound each)

3 tablespoons olive oil

1 large onion, finely chopped

2 large carrots, peeled and shredded

2 stalks celery, finely chopped

1 quart homemade or canned low-sodium chicken broth

1 clove garlic, minced

¼ teaspoon salt

¼ teaspoon freshly ground black pepper

¼ teaspoon freshly grated nutmeg

¾ cup whole milk or half-and-half

1 cup (4 ounces) shredded extra-sharp Cheddar cheese or Gruyère cheese

⅓ cup dry white wine

½ cup Garlic Sourdough Croutons (page 52)

Preheat the oven to 375°F. With a small, sharp knife, cut wide tops out of the pumpkins to make bowls. Scrape out and discard the seeds and fibers. Replace the tops and arrange the pumpkins on a parchment-lined baking sheet. Bake until tender when pierced with a knife but still firm, 40 to 45 minutes. Let cool slightly. Trim all but ¼ inch of flesh from the tops, reserving the trimmed flesh. Cut and scrape out some of the flesh of each pumpkin to make shells with about a ¾-cup capacity. Dice the trimmed flesh and set aside.

Meanwhile, heat 2 tablespoons of the oil in a large saucepan over medium heat. Add the onion, carrots, and celery and sauté until translucent, 8 to 10 minutes. Add the broth, garlic, salt, pepper, and nutmeg. Cover and simmer for 20 minutes, or until the vegetables are tender. Let cool slightly. Working in 2 or 3 batches, in a blender or food processor fitted with the metal blade, process the vegetable mixture to a purée. Return the purée to the saucepan. Stir in the milk and cook until heated through. Add the cheese and wine and cook, stirring, until the cheese melts. Taste and adjust the seasoning.

Heat the remaining 1 tablespoon oil over medium heat. Add the cooked squash pieces and toss and stir just to heat through. Place the hot pumpkin tureens on dinner plates and ladle in the soup. Sprinkle with croutons. Serve immediately, with the sautéed pumpkin alongside to spoon over the soup.

Gingered Yellow Squash Soup

Partner this spicy soup with crispy flatbread or focaccia. A spoonful of bright green dill or basil pesto makes a dazzling accent to behold and savor. SERVES 4

1 tablespoon olive oil

1 medium onion, chopped

2 cloves garlic, minced

1 tablespoon minced peeled fresh ginger

¾ teaspoon salt

¼ teaspoon ground cumin

¼ teaspoon ground turmeric

⅛ teaspoon freshly ground black pepper

Pinch of cayenne pepper

5 medium yellow straight- or crookneck squash (about 1½ pounds total)

2 plum (Roma) tomatoes, peeled, seeded, and chopped (see Note)

3 cups homemade or canned low-sodium chicken broth

½ cup plain yogurt

Dill Pesto for serving (recipe follows)

In a large saucepan, heat the oil over medium heat. Add the onion, garlic, and ginger and sauté until soft, 8 minutes. Add the salt, cumin, turmeric, black pepper, and cayenne and sauté for 2 minutes longer. Add the squash, tomatoes, and broth. Bring to a boil over high heat, then reduce the heat to low, cover, and simmer until the squash is tender when pierced with a knife, about 15 minutes.

Remove from the heat and let cool slightly. In a blender or food processor fitted with the metal blade, process the soup to a smooth purée. Add the yogurt and pulse just to blend. Taste and adjust the seasoning. Serve hot or cold: Return to the pan and gently reheat until warmed throughout if needed; or refrigerate until thoroughly chilled, about 2 hours. Ladle into bowls and garnish with a spoonful of the pesto.

NOTE: To peel tomatoes, score an X in the blossom end of each, then plunge them into a pot of boiling water and cook until the skins begin to wrinkle, 20 to 30 seconds. Using tongs, transfer the tomatoes to a bowl of ice water. As soon as they cool, remove from the water and peel away the skins, using your fingers or a small, sharp knife. To seed a tomato, cut it in half crosswise, then lightly squeeze and shake it to dislodge the seeds. Use a finger if needed to help dislodge the seed sacs.

continued >

Dill Pesto

MAKES ¾ CUP

1½ cups packed fresh dill leaves

½ cup packed fresh flat-leaf
   (Italian) parsley

2 tablespoons pistachios or pine nuts

2 large cloves garlic, minced

3 to 4 tablespoons extra-virgin
   olive oil

2 tablespoons freshly grated
   Parmesan cheese

In a blender or food processor fitted with the metal blade, combine the dill, parsley, nuts, and garlic. Process until finely minced. Add the oil and cheese and process until blended. Transfer to a small bowl, cover, and chill. Bring to room temperature before using if serving the soup hot.

Moroccan Meatball, Chard, and Kabocha Squash Soup

This colorful soup makes a nourishing full meal with crusty sourdough bread, an arugula and goat cheese salad, and Caramel-Glazed Pumpkin-Date Bars (page 74) for dessert. Substitute butternut squash or sugar pumpkin if kabocha isn't available. SERVES 6 TO 8

MEATBALLS:

1 pound lean ground lamb or
   ground chuck

3 tablespoons cornstarch

1 large egg

3 tablespoons minced fresh cilantro

½ teaspoon ground allspice

1 clove garlic, minced

1 bunch red Swiss chard
   (about 12 ounces)

1 tablespoon olive oil

1 medium onion, finely chopped

1 carrot, peeled and shredded

1 stalk fennel or celery, chopped

2 teaspoons grated peeled fresh
   ginger

½ teaspoon ground allspice

½ teaspoon ground cumin

½ teaspoon freshly ground black
   pepper

1½ quarts beef broth

2 cups diced kabocha squash
   (⅜-inch dice)

5 tablespoons tomato paste

6 red or yellow plum (Roma)
   tomatoes, sliced

Salt to taste

¼ cup chopped fresh cilantro

To make the meatballs, in a bowl, combine the lamb, cornstarch, egg, cilantro, allspice, and garlic and mix lightly. Shape into ¾-inch balls.

Remove the ribs from the Swiss chard and slice thinly crosswise. Chop the leaves separately; set aside. In a large pot, heat the oil over medium heat. Add the chard ribs, onion, carrot, and fennel and sauté until limp. Add the ginger, allspice, cumin, pepper, broth, squash, and tomato paste; bring to a boil. Reduce the heat to low, cover, and simmer for 10 minutes. Using a slotted spoon, carefully drop the meatballs into the hot broth. Add the chard leaves and tomatoes. Simmer for 5 or 6 minutes longer, or until the vegetables are tender and the meatballs are cooked through. Season with salt.

Ladle into bowls, sprinkle with the cilantro, and serve immediately.

Sesame, Quinoa, Butternut Squash, and Pear Salad

Quinoa is the only grain that furnishes a complete protein. Here it provides the backdrop for a tantalizing autumn salad. Serve as a side dish, or partner with a crusty artisanal bread, such as sourdough, cheese, or olive, for an excellent midday meal. SERVES 4

1½ cups diced butternut squash or
    pumpkin (½-inch dice)

½ cup quinoa

1½ cups water

2 teaspoons soy sauce

1 teaspoon sesame oil

½ teaspoon ground cinnamon

¼ teaspoon ground allspice

Salt and freshly ground black pepper
    to taste

1 Comice pear, halved, cored, and
    diced (½-inch dice)

12 oil-packed sun-dried tomatoes,
    drained and halved

2 tablespoons balsamic vinegar

1 teaspoon Dijon mustard

3 tablespoons olive oil

⅓ roasted pistachios

1 cup arugula

Place the squash in a shallow baking dish, cover with plastic wrap, and microwave on high for 7 to 8 minutes, or until tender when pierced with a knife. Let cool to room temperature.

In a medium saucepan, combine the quinoa, water, soy sauce, sesame oil, cinnamon, allspice, and salt and pepper. Bring to a boil over medium-high heat, then reduce the heat to low, cover, and simmer for 10 minutes. Remove from the heat and let stand for 10 minutes; fluff with a fork. Let cool almost to room temperature. Gently fold in the squash, pear, and tomatoes.

In a small bowl, whisk together the vinegar, mustard, and olive oil; spoon over the quinoa mixture and toss lightly. Arrange the salad on a platter or individual plates and serve warm or chilled. Sprinkle with the pistachios and arugula just before serving.

Delicata Squash Rings
with Arugula, Fuyu Persimmon, Dried Cranberries, and Feta

The delicata squash is very quick cooking and when finished attains a caramel glaze from the natural sugar in the flesh. Serve the squash slightly warm with this cool salad topping. It makes for a striking presentation and taste. SERVES 6

2 delicata squash (about ½ pound each)

1½ tablespoons olive oil

Salt and freshly ground black pepper to taste

BALSAMIC VINAIGRETTE:

3 tablespoons extra-virgin olive oil

1 teaspoon Dijon mustard

1 tablespoon freshly squeezed lemon juice

1 tablespoon balsamic vinegar

Salt and freshly ground black pepper to taste

8 cups mixed field greens, arugula, or mesclun

1 unpeeled Fuyu persimmon or Fuji apple, halved, cored, and thinly sliced

⅓ cup dried cranberries

3 ounces feta cheese, crumbled

Peel the squash with a vegetable peeler. Slice off the ends and scoop out the seeds to create hollow cylinders. Cut the squash into rings about ⅓ inch thick. In a large, wide skillet, heat the olive oil over medium heat. Add the squash rings and cook until the rings are lightly browned on the first side, about 6 minutes; turn and cook the second sides until tender when pierced with a knife, 5 to 6 minutes longer.

Transfer the rings to a platter or individual plates and let cool slightly. Season with salt and pepper.

To make the vinaigrette, in a large bowl, whisk together the extra-virgin olive oil, mustard, lemon juice, vinegar, and salt and pepper. Add the greens and toss lightly. Spoon into the center of the squash rings and garnish with the persimmon slices. Sprinkle with the cranberries and feta and serve.

Roasted Butternut Squash Polenta with Fried Sage

Roasting caramelizes the sugars and brings out the sweetness of the tender chunks of butternut squash that punctuate this golden yellow polenta casserole. It is finished off with the herbal overtones of butter-browned sage. SERVES 6

1-pound piece butternut squash or
    sugar pumpkin, peeled, seeded,
    and cut into ½-inch dice

3 tablespoons olive oil

1 cup polenta

1½ cups cold water

2 cups homemade or canned
    low-sodium chicken broth

½ teaspoon salt

¼ teaspoon freshly ground black
    pepper

2 tablespoons butter

12 fresh sage leaves, chopped

⅓ cup (1½ ounces) freshly grated
    Pecorino Romano or Parmesan
    cheese

Preheat the oven to 400°F. Line a baking sheet with parchment paper. In a bowl, toss the squash with 2 tablespoons of the oil and spread on the prepared pan. Bake for 15 minutes. Stir and turn the squash, and continue baking until tender when pierced with a knife, 15 to 20 minutes longer.

Meanwhile, in a medium bowl, soak the polenta in the cold water for 10 minutes. In a large saucepan, bring the broth to a boil over high heat. Stir in the polenta and any remaining water, the salt, pepper, and remaining 1 tablespoon oil. Return to a boil, then reduce the heat to low and simmer, stirring occasionally, until thickened, about 15 minutes. Stir the squash into the polenta and cook until heated through. Spoon into a hot bowl for serving.

In a small saucepan, melt the butter over medium heat and cook until it sizzles and browns lightly, then add the sage and sauté until crisp. Scatter over the polenta. Sprinkle with the cheese and serve at once.

Goat Cheese—Stuffed Squash Blossom
and Heirloom Tomato Salad

Brilliant yellow squash blossoms nestle in this peppery arugula salad for a dramatic first course.
I love ducking into the garden to pick the blossoms in the early morning hours and gather some tomato
heirlooms: Marvel Stripe, Green Zebra, and Brandywine varieties are perfect for this. The farmers'
market also yields these beauties; in some regions you can find them until late November or
December. SERVES 4

8 large squash blossoms

2 tablespoons finely chopped fresh
basil

1 tablespoon finely chopped fresh
chives

3 ounces soft goat cheese, in a log

1 large egg, lightly beaten

2 teaspoons water

⅓ cup all-purpose flour

2 tablespoons olive oil

LEMON VINAIGRETTE:

3 tablespoons extra-virgin olive oil

1 teaspoon Dijon mustard

1 tablespoon freshly squeezed
lemon juice

1 tablespoon white wine vinegar

Salt and freshly ground black pepper
to taste

4 ounces arugula (about 8 cups)

1 pound heirloom tomatoes, cored
and sliced

Fresh basil sprigs for garnish

Remove and discard the stems from the squash blossoms. Sprinkle the herbs all over the goat cheese, patting to help them adhere, and cut it into 8 cubes. Place a piece of herb-coated cheese in each squash blossom and twist to close.

In a small dish, combine the egg and water. Put the flour in another bowl. Dip a blossom in the egg mixture, then roll in the flour to coat; set aside on a plate. Repeat to coat the remaining stuffed blossoms. Heat the olive oil in a large skillet over medium-high heat. Place the squash blossoms in the skillet and cook, turning occasionally, for 3 to 4 minutes, or until golden brown. Transfer to paper towels to drain. Keep warm in a low oven.

To make the vinaigrette, in a large bowl, whisk together the extra-virgin olive oil, mustard, lemon juice, vinegar, and salt and pepper. Add the arugula and toss lightly. Divide among individual plates. Arrange the tomatoes on top and garnish with the squash blossoms and basil. Serve immediately.

Acorn Squash Halves with Orange Pecans

This oven-baked, sweet and nutty side dish makes a pretty accompaniment for roast pork or turkey.

SERVES 4

2 medium acorn squash, halved
    lengthwise and seeded
3 tablespoons butter, at room
    temperature
2 tablespoons lightly packed brown
    sugar
½ teaspoon ground cinnamon
1 tablespoon grated orange zest
¼ cup freshly squeezed orange juice
½ cup pecans

Preheat the oven to 375°F. Place the squash, cut side down, in a large, shallow baking dish and fill with water to come ½ inch up the sides. Bake until tender when pierced with a knife, about 40 minutes.

Turn the squash cut side up and place in a clean baking dish. In a small bowl, cream together the butter, brown sugar, cinnamon, and orange zest and juice; mix in the nuts. Divide the butter mixture evenly among the squash cavities. Continue baking uncovered until lightly browned, about 20 minutes longer. Serve hot.

Mashed Squash Variation: Bake the squash as directed above. Let cool for a few minutes, then scoop the flesh from the shell. Place in a bowl, mash, and mix in the butter, cinnamon, and orange zest and juice. Pile in a baking dish and sprinkle with the pecans and brown sugar. Continue baking, uncovered, until the pecans are lightly toasted, about 20 minutes longer.

Roasted Autumn Root Vegetables

Most vegetables develop a tantalizing caramelized sweetness when oven-roasted, and root vegetables are exceptional candidates for this easy preparation. They are delicious hot from the oven; they also reheat well if you wish to do a large batch at once. MAKES 8 TO 10 SERVINGS

1 winter squash such as butternut, kabocha, banana, or Hubbard (about 1½ pounds), peeled, seeded, and cut into ½-inch wedges about 2 inches long

8 small Yukon Gold potatoes, scrubbed and quartered or cut into ½-inch wedges

1 large onion, cut into ½-inch wedges

3 slender carrots, peeled and cut into 1½-inch lengths

3 slender parsnips, peeled and cut into 1½-inch lengths

2 tablespoons olive oil

1 tablespoon balsamic vinegar

Fresh thyme or oregano leaves or minced fresh sage for garnish

Preheat the oven to 400°F. Line a baking sheet with parchment paper. In a large bowl, combine the squash, potatoes, onion, carrots, and parsnips. Pour over the oil and vinegar and toss to mix and coat. Spread out on the prepared pan.

Bake for 15 minutes. Stir and turn the vegetables, and continue baking until tender when pierced with a knife, 30 to 35 minutes longer, stirring once or twice. Sprinkle with the herbs and serve.

Gold and green summer squash and vivid orange pumpkin and
winter squash contribute a bright harmony and succulent flavor to these
hearty main dishes. Pumpkins and squash complement a gallery of centerpiece
dishes from pasta to chicken and fish to pork, lamb, and beef,
all easy to add to your collection for tantalizing dining.

Entrées

SUGAR PUMPKIN–WHITE CHEDDAR CHEESE SOUFFLÉ WITH GARLIC SOURDOUGH CROUTONS 52

TORTELLINI WITH BUTTERNUT SQUASH, ARTICHOKE HEARTS, AND PECORINO 54

SPAGHETTI SQUASH WITH SPICY MEAT SAUCE 57

CHAYOTE STUFFED WITH LAMB AND PINE NUTS 59

FIVE-SPICE PORK TENDERLOIN WITH PUMPKIN HALF-MOONS AND RED GRAPES 60

ORZO WITH YELLOW SQUASH, LEEKS, AND SUN-DRIED TOMATOES 62

LAMB CHOPS, SUMMER SQUASH, AND ONIONS BANDIT STYLE 63

BEEF, SQUASH, AND ONIONS IN RED WINE WITH RICE PILAF 64

TILAPIA TAHINI ON GREEN AND GOLD SQUASH STRIPS 65

LEMON-ROASTED CHICKEN WITH GARLIC, WINTER SQUASH, APPLES, AND ONIONS 67

CURRIED CHICKEN WITH BUTTERNUT SQUASH CRESCENTS AND POMEGRANATE SEEDS 69

GRILLED CHICKEN BREASTS STUFFED WITH ZUCCHINI AND GOAT CHEESE 70

Sugar Pumpkin—White Cheddar Cheese Soufflé
with Garlic Sourdough Croutons

Garlicky sourdough croutons spark this soufflé enriched with pumpkin and cheese. A green salad embellished with Comice pears or Fuyu persimmons and toasted hazelnuts or pecans would be a simple but lavish complementary pairing. SERVES 4

GARLIC SOURDOUGH CROUTONS:

1 clove garlic, minced

1 tablespoon olive oil

2 slices sourdough French bread, cut into ½-inch cubes (about 1¼ cups)

4 eggs, separated, plus 1 egg white

¾ cup pumpkin or winter squash purée, canned or homemade

⅓ cup sour cream or heavy (whipping) cream

¼ teaspoon salt

1 teaspoon Italian herbs or *herbes de Provence*

1 teaspoon ground cinnamon

¼ teaspoon freshly grated nutmeg

1 cup (4 ounces) shredded sharp white Cheddar cheese

¼ teaspoon cream of tartar

Preheat the oven to 375°F. Butter and flour a 4-cup soufflé dish.

To make the croutons, in a small baking dish, combine the garlic and oil, stir to coat, and let steep for a few minutes. Add the croutons and toss to coat. Bake for 5 minutes, or until lightly toasted; set aside.

In a large bowl, whisk the egg yolks until lightened in color. Stir in the pumpkin, sour cream, salt, herbs, cinnamon, and nutmeg. Mix in ¾ cup of the cheese.

In a large bowl, using an electric mixer set on medium-high speed, beat the 5 egg whites until foamy. Add the cream of tartar and beat until stiff, glossy peaks form. Fold one-fourth of the egg whites into the pumpkin mixture. Fold this mixture and half the garlic croutons into the remaining egg whites. Spoon into the prepared dish. Sprinkle the remaining croutons and ¼ cup cheese on top.

Bake until set and golden brown, 25 to 30 minutes. Serve immediately.

Tortellini
with Butternut Squash, Artichoke Hearts, and Pecorino

This hearty pasta dish is excellent hot, or serve it at room temperature for a salad entrée. Accompany with an artisan herb or olive bread and greens tossed in a vinaigrette. For dessert, savor a slice of Five-Spice Pumpkin-Ginger Cake (page 79). SERVES 8 TO 10

12 ounces tortellini

1-pound piece butternut or kabocha squash or sugar pumpkin, seeded

1 cup red cherry tomatoes, halved

1 jar (6 ounces) marinated artichoke hearts, cut into ½-inch chunks

⅓ cup olive oil

⅓ cup freshly grated Pecorino Romano cheese

½ cup toasted pine nuts or pistachios

Bring a large saucepan three-fourths full of lightly salted water to a boil. Add the tortellini and cook until al dente, 10 to 12 minutes.

Meanwhile, place the squash in a baking dish, cover with plastic wrap, and microwave on high for 7 to 8 minutes, or until tender when pierced with a knife. Scoop out the flesh and cut into ⅜-inch dice.

Drain the pasta and turn out into a warmed bowl. Add the squash, tomatoes, artichoke hearts, oil, and cheese. Toss to mix, and sprinkle with the nuts. Serve at room temperature or refrigerate until serving time.

Spaghetti Squash with Spicy Meat Sauce

When baked and fluffed with a fork, the interior of the spaghetti squash separates into strands just like the pasta. Here it makes a succulent cushion for a spicy meat sauce to adorn with avocado, red and yellow cherry tomatoes, and shavings of Parmesan. Serve the medley in the squash shell for a dramatic table centerpiece. SERVES 8

GREEK MEAT SAUCE:

2 tablespoons olive oil

1 large onion, chopped

1½ pounds ground beef or turkey

1 cup water

1½ cans (9 ounces) tomato paste

2 tablespoons red wine vinegar

2 cloves garlic, minced

1 teaspoon salt

Freshly ground black pepper to taste

1 teaspoon whole mixed pickling
   spice

½ stick cinnamon

1 large spaghetti squash
   (about 3 pounds)

¼ teaspoon salt

¼ teaspoon freshly ground black
   pepper

4 tablespoons (½ stick) unsalted
   butter

1 avocado, pitted, peeled, and diced

12 cherry tomatoes, red or yellow
   or a combination, halved

½ cup fresh Parmesan or Pecorino
   Romano cheese shavings

2 tablespoons chopped fresh flat-leaf
   (Italian) parsley

To make the Greek Meat Sauce, in a large saucepan, heat 1 tablespoon of the oil over medium heat. Add the onion and sauté until translucent, about 5 minutes. Transfer the onion to a plate, leaving the oil in the pan. Brown the meat in the reserved oil over medium-high heat, stirring to break it up into even crumbles. Return the onion to the pan. Add the water, tomato paste, vinegar, garlic, salt, and pepper. Tie the pickling spice and cinnamon in a small piece of cheesecloth and add to the stew. Reduce the heat to low, cover, and simmer for 1 hour, stirring occasionally and adding additional water if it threatens to scorch. Discard the cheesecloth.

Preheat the oven to 350°F. Line a baking sheet with parchment paper. Cut the squash in half lengthwise and scoop out the seeds. Place the squash, cut side down, on the prepared pan. Bake until the flesh can be easily scraped into strands with a fork, 50 to 70 minutes. Remove from the oven and let cool slightly. Using a fork, scoop out all the flesh into a bowl and fluff the spaghetti-like strands. Toss in the salt and pepper. Place on a large, warmed platter or the cleaned squash shell.

Melt the butter in a small saucepan over medium heat and cook until it turns light brown. Pour over the squash strands. Toss with the fork to blend. Top the squash with the hot meat sauce. Scatter the avocado and tomatoes over and sprinkle with the cheese and parsley. Serve immediately.

Chayote Stuffed with Lamb and Pine Nuts

Chayote half-shells make charming edible containers for serving a spicy ground lamb skillet dish. Accompany with cracked wheat and a tomato, cucumber, feta, and olive salad for a Middle East repast. SERVES 4

4 medium chayote squash (about
    3 pounds total), halved lengthwise
    and seeded
1 tablespoon canola oil
1 small yellow onion or 4 green
    onions, including tender green
    tops, chopped
2 cloves garlic, minced
1 pound ground lamb
⅓ cup tomato sauce
4 tablespoons pine nuts
½ teaspoon ground cumin
½ teaspoon ground allspice
½ teaspoon salt
Freshly ground black pepper to taste
2 tablespoons unsalted butter
1½ cups (6 ounces) shredded
    Monterey Jack cheese

Place the chayote halves in a large saucepan with lightly salted water just to cover. Bring to a boil over medium-high heat. Reduce the heat to low, cover, and simmer until tender when pierced with a knife, 15 to 20 minutes; drain. Carefully scoop out the pulp, leaving a thin, firm shell. Chop the pulp finely, then turn out into a colander to drain off any excess liquid.

Preheat the oven to 350°F. Oil a large baking sheet.

In a large skillet over medium heat, heat the oil. Add the onion and sauté until soft, 8 minutes. Add the garlic, crumble in the meat, and continue to cook until the meat is well browned, about 5 minutes. Add the tomato sauce, nuts, cumin, allspice, salt, pepper, and chayote pulp. Continue to cook for 10 to 15 minutes, letting the juices evaporate. Lightly fill the chayote shells with the mixture. Dot with the butter and sprinkle with the cheese. Place on the baking sheet. Bake until hot throughout, about 15 minutes. Serve hot.

Five-Spice Pork Tenderloin
with Pumpkin Half-Moons and Red Grapes

The tantalizing flavor of Chinese five-spice powder—with its licorice overtone—gilds pork in a soy-and-sesame-based glaze with a marvelous aroma and taste. Crescents of roasted pumpkin or squash and wine-steeped grapes complete a sweet, savory, and very picturesque platter. SERVES 6

SOY-SESAME MARINADE:

2 tablespoons soy sauce

2 tablespoons dry sherry

1 teaspoon Chinese five-spice powder

1½ teaspoons minced peeled fresh
   ginger

1 clove garlic, minced

1 teaspoon sesame oil

1 pork tenderloin (about 1¼ pounds)

2 tablespoons olive oil

1 tablespoon balsamic vinegar

1½ pounds sugar pumpkin or winter
   squash such as butternut, kabocha,
   buttercup, or Hubbard, peeled,
   seeded, and cut into half-moons
   about ⅜ inch thick

1 tablespoon unsalted butter

1½ cups (10 ounces) red seedless
   grapes

¼ cup dry sherry

To make the marinade, in a small bowl, combine the soy sauce, sherry, five-spice powder, ginger, garlic, and sesame oil.

Place the pork tenderloin in a baking dish or lock-top plastic bag. Pour the marinade over. Cover or seal and refrigerate for at least 2 hours or up to overnight, turning several times.

Preheat the oven to 400°F. Position one rack in the middle of the oven and a second rack in the lower third of the oven. Line a baking sheet with parchment paper.

In a bowl, whisk together the olive oil and vinegar. Add the pumpkin and toss to coat. Place on the prepared sheet and place on the lower rack of the oven. Bake for 30 minutes.

Place the meat on a rack in a roasting pan (reserve the marinade). Place in the oven on the middle rack and roast until an instant-read thermometer inserted into the center registers 145°F, 15 to 20 minutes, basting occasionally with the remaining marinade. Continue roasting the pumpkin until tender when pierced with a knife, 40 to 45 minutes total.

Transfer the meat to a carving board, tent with aluminum foil, and let rest for 5 minutes. Meanwhile, in a small skillet, melt the butter over medium heat. Add the grapes and heat for about 1 minute. Pour in the sherry and cook until the liquid is reduced to 2 tablespoons. Carve the pork and transfer to a platter. Surround with the pumpkin and grapes, and serve.

Orzo with Yellow Squash, Leeks,
and Sun-Dried Tomatoes

This colorful pasta medley makes a welcome, quick-to-assemble entrée for the short days of fall and winter, served hot from the pan. In warmer weather, enjoy it at room temperature or chilled.

SERVES 4 TO 6

8 ounces (1⅓ cups) orzo pasta

3 tablespoons olive oil

1 leek, white part only, chopped

2 yellow straight- or crookneck squash (about 1 pound total), cut into ⅓-inch dice

3 tablespoons freshly squeezed lemon juice

1 shallot or green onion, finely chopped

1½ tablespoons minced fresh dill or 1 teaspoon dried dill

2 teaspoons minced fresh oregano or ½ teaspoon dried oregano

Salt and freshly ground black pepper to taste

½ cup oil-packed sun-dried tomatoes, drained and snipped into small pieces

½ cup (2 ounces) crumbled feta cheese

¼ cup minced fresh flat-leaf (Italian) parsley

Arugula leaves for serving

Bring a large saucepan three-fourths full of lightly salted water to a boil. Add the orzo and cook until al dente, 12 to 15 minutes; drain, letting some of the cooking liquid cling to the pasta. Let cool for a few minutes.

Meanwhile, in a skillet over medium heat, heat 1 tablespoon of the oil. Add the leek and squash and sauté until soft, about 3 minutes.

In a bowl, stir together the remaining 2 tablespoons oil, the lemon juice, shallot, dill, oregano, and salt and pepper. Add the pasta and toss to coat. Stir in the squash mixture, tomatoes, feta, and parsley. Serve warm or at room temperature, or refrigerate until thoroughly chilled, about 3 hours, if you like. When ready to serve, tuck the arugula around the edge of the serving bowl or individual plates.

Lamb Chops, Summer Squash, and Onions
Bandit Style

In Greek tradition, the meat and vegetables are sealed and cooked "bandit style," or wrapped in a parchment-paper pouch. For a charming first course, start with stuffed grape leaves and Kalamata olives. Accompany with the typical country salad of tomatoes, cucumbers, feta, and olives. SERVES 2

2 lamb sirloin chops (about
  1¼ pounds total)
2 teaspoons minced fresh oregano or
  ½ teaspoon crumbled dried
  oregano
1 clove garlic, minced
Salt and freshly ground black pepper
  to taste
2 small pattypan squash, sliced
  crosswise ⅜ inch thick
2 baby yellow straight- or crookneck
  squash (about 4 inches each),
  halved lengthwise
2 green onions, chopped
2 ounces feta cheese
1½ tablespoons freshly squeezed
  lemon juice
1 tablespoon olive oil

Preheat the oven to 350°F.

Season the lamb chops with the oregano, garlic, and salt and pepper. Place each on a 12-inch-long sheet of parchment paper or aluminum foil. Divide the pattypan and yellow squash on top. Scatter on the onions and crumble over the cheese, again dividing evenly. Drizzle each serving with the lemon juice and oil. Fold the parchment or foil over the top, line up the ends, and double-fold the top seam and then the sides; secure each edge with paper clips.

Place the packets on a baking sheet and bake until the meat is cooked through, about 30 minutes. To test for doneness, open a corner of a packet and insert an instant-read thermometer into the meat; it should register 145°F for medium-rare. To serve, place the sealed packets on dinner plates and allow guests to open them themselves; fragrant steam will rise to greet them.

Beef, Squash, and Onions in Red Wine
with Rice Pilaf

This Greek dish is a superb make-ahead entrée for guests. The stew can be made a day in advance;
the flavors will mellow even further. SERVES 6

1 tablespoon unsalted butter

3 medium onions, cut into wedges

2 tablespoons olive oil

2 pounds beef stew meat, cut into
   2-inch chunks

1 cup dry red wine

3 tablespoons red wine vinegar

¼ cup tomato paste

3 cloves garlic, minced

1 tablespoon brown sugar

¾ teaspoon salt

2 teaspoons whole mixed pickling
   spice

1 stick cinnamon

1 butternut, kabocha, or buttercup
   squash (1½ pounds), peeled,
   seeded, and cut into 1-inch squares
   ½ inch thick

RICE PILAF:

2½ cups water

1¼ cups basmati rice

½ teaspoon salt

1 teaspoon ground cinnamon

¼ cup unsalted butter

3 tablespoons pine nuts

In a large Dutch oven or saucepan, melt the butter over medium heat. Add the onions and sauté until barely golden, about 10 minutes. Transfer the onions to a plate. Add the oil and brown the meat cubes well. Return the onions to the pot and stir in the wine, vinegar, tomato paste, garlic, sugar, and salt. Tie the pickling spice and cinnamon in a small piece of cheesecloth and add to the stew. Reduce the heat to low, cover, and simmer for 1 hour, or until the meat is almost tender, stirring occasionally and adding additional water if it threatens to scorch. Add the squash to the pot and simmer for 20 minutes longer, or until the meat and squash are tender.

Meanwhile, make the pilaf: In a large saucepan, bring the water to a boil. Add the rice, salt, and cinnamon. Reduce the heat to low, cover, and simmer until the rice is just tender, about 15 minutes. In a small saucepan, melt the butter over medium-high heat and cook until it bubbles and turns golden brown. Pour over the rice and sprinkle with the pine nuts. (Toss the nuts in the butter pan during the last minute, if you wish.)

Serve the rice alongside the stew.

Tilapia Tahini on Green and Gold Squash Strips

Ribbons of zucchini and yellow squash make a neat cushion for broiled fish fillets sealed in a lemon-kissed sesame sauce. SERVES 4

2 medium zucchini, ends trimmed, sliced lengthwise ⅜ inch thick

2 yellow straight-neck squash, ends trimmed, sliced lengthwise ⅜ inch thick

Olive oil for brushing

4 large tilapia or catfish fillets (about 6 ounces each)

Salt and white pepper

2 tablespoons unsalted butter

1 clove garlic, minced

3 tablespoons tahini (see Note)

3 tablespoons freshly squeezed lemon juice

2 tablespoons chopped fresh mint, basil, or flat-leaf (Italian) parsley, plus sprigs for garnish

Preheat the oven to 450°F. Line a baking sheet with parchment paper. Place the squash in a shallow dish and brush with oil to coat. Place on the prepared pan in a single layer. Bake for 10 minutes, or until crisp-tender. Set aside and keep warm.

Preheat the broiler. Place the fish on a broiling pan; season with salt and pepper. In a small saucepan, melt the butter with the garlic over medium heat and drizzle over the fish. Broil on one side only, until the fish is golden brown and flakes easily when prodded with a fork, about 4 minutes.

While the fish is cooking, in a small bowl, mix together the tahini, lemon juice, and chopped mint. Arrange the squash on dinner plates, dividing it evenly. Place a fish fillet on top of each bed of squash. Spoon the tahini sauce over the fish. Garnish with the herb sprigs and serve at once.

NOTE: Tahini is a sesame seed paste available in natural-foods stores, the gourmet section of supermarkets, or Mediterranean markets.

Trout Variation: Instead of using tilapia or catfish fillets, arrange two whole 1-pound trout on a parchment-lined baking sheet. Bake in a preheated 425°F oven until opaque throughout, about 20 minutes. Skin and fillet the trout. Arrange each half on a squash bed. Top with the tahini sauce.

Lemon-Roasted Chicken
with Garlic, Winter Squash, Apples, and Onions

Ideally season the bird for this flavorful rendition with salt, lemon juice, and garlic a day ahead, or at least several hours in advance. The chicken is then roasted with comfort-food accompaniments for an easy, delectable, hearty dinner. Serve with an arugula, red grape, and Gorgonzola salad and finish off with Candied Ginger–Pumpkin Crème Brûlée (page 88) for a menu to regale guests.

SERVES 4 TO 5

1 whole frying chicken
   (3½ to 4 pounds)

Sea salt

8 cloves garlic, slivered

1 lemon, halved and seeded

Freshly ground black pepper

2 tablespoons olive oil, plus extra
   for drizzling

1½ tablespoons balsamic vinegar

1 large winter squash such as
   butternut, banana, kabocha, or
   Hubbard (1½ pounds), peeled,
   seeded, and cut into 1½-inch
   squares ½ inch thick

3 Granny Smith, Golden Delicious, or
   Jonathan apples, halved, cored,
   and each cut into eight wedges

2 unpeeled Fuyu persimmons, halved,
   cored, and each cut into eight
   wedges (optional)

1 large onion, cut into wedges

1 head garlic

Wash and pat dry the chicken. Season the chicken lightly inside and out with sea salt. Loosen the breast skin with your fingers and insert the garlic underneath, distributing it evenly. Squeeze the lemon juice over the surface and tuck the halves inside the cavity. Season inside and out with black pepper. Place in a baking dish, cover with plastic wrap, and refrigerate for several hours, or preferably overnight.

Preheat the oven to 375°F. (Use a convection oven if available.) Line a baking dish with parchment paper. Place the chicken on a rack in a roasting pan and let it come to room temperature.

Combine the 2 tablespoons oil and vinegar in a large bowl. Add the squash and toss lightly to coat. Arrange the squash in the roasting pan around the chicken. Toss the apples, persimmon, and onion in the remaining oil mixture and place in the prepared baking dish. Slice ¼ inch off the top of the head of garlic; place on a small sheet of aluminum foil and drizzle lightly with oil. Wrap to enclose and place in the roasting pan with the chicken.

continued >

Roast the chicken and the apple-onion dish for 30 minutes. Check the apples and onions, testing for doneness by piercing with a knife. If tender, remove the apples and onions from the oven; if not, return to the oven and check frequently until done. Continue to roast the chicken and squash 30 to 40 minutes longer, or until an instant-read thermometer inserted in the thickest part of a thigh registers 175°F. Transfer the chicken to a large platter and surround with the squash, apples, persimmon, and onions; open the garlic packet, peel the cloves, and scatter around the platter. Carve the chicken and serve.

Curried Chicken
with Butternut Squash Crescents and Pomegranate Seeds

Mango chutney, spices, and orange juice mingle to create a flavor-packed glaze for chicken quarters. Choose a slender, more elongated butternut squash for slicing into pretty half-moons. Serve this entrée with its pretty scarlet seeds as an eye-catching main course for company. SERVES 4

1 pound butternut squash, peeled,
   seeded, and halved lengthwise
1½ tablespoons olive oil
1 tablespoon balsamic vinegar
4 chicken leg-and-thigh quarters
Salt and freshly ground black pepper
   to taste
1 cup freshly squeezed orange juice
½ cup homemade or canned
   low-sodium chicken broth
½ cup mango chutney
⅓ cup golden raisins
1½ teaspoons Madras curry powder
1 teaspoon ground cinnamon
Pomegranate seeds for garnish
   (about ½ cup)

Preheat the oven to 375°F. Line a baking sheet with parchment paper.

Cut the squash halves crosswise into slices about ⅜ inch thick to make half-moons, then in half again to make crescents. Whisk together the oil and vinegar in a medium bowl. Add the squash and toss to coat. Arrange on the prepared pan. Place the chicken in a buttered baking dish and sprinkle with salt and pepper. Bake the chicken and squash for 15 minutes.

Meanwhile, in a small saucepan over medium heat, combine the orange juice, broth, chutney, raisins, curry powder, and cinnamon and simmer until slightly thickened, about 10 minutes. Pour the sauce over the chicken and continue baking, basting frequently, until an instant-read thermometer inserted in the thickest part of a thigh registers 175°F, 30 to 40 minutes longer. Bake the squash until tender when pierced with a knife. Arrange the chicken and squash on individual plates and serve hot, garnished with the pomegranate seeds.

Grilled Chicken Breasts Stuffed
with Zucchini and Goat Cheese

Here a creamy, moist zucchini spread lies beneath the skin of golden brown barbecued chicken breasts. These are easy to assemble in advance, refrigerate, and grill just before dinner. Accompany with grilled corn on the cob and heirloom tomato and mozzarella salad, and finish off with Honey-Rum Pumpkin Ice Cream (page 87). Don't put your grill away at the end of summer; the smoky flavor of grilled foods is perfect for chilly days as well. SERVES 4

1 pound zucchini

Salt

2 tablespoons extra-virgin olive oil, plus extra for brushing

1 medium onion, finely chopped

4 ounces goat cheese, at room temperature

3 tablespoons unsalted butter, at room temperature

1 large egg

2 tablespoons minced flat-leaf (Italian) parsley

⅓ cup freshly grated Parmesan cheese

4 bone-in, skin-on chicken breast halves (about 12 ounces each)

Herbes de Provence for sprinkling

Prepare a charcoal grill for a medium-hot fire, preheat a gas grill to medium-high, or preheat the oven to 375°F.

Shred the zucchini, sprinkle with salt, wrap in paper towels, and let stand for 15 minutes. Squeeze the zucchini dry. In a large skillet, heat 1 tablespoon of the oil over medium heat. Add the zucchini and sauté until crisp-tender, 2 to 3 minutes; remove from the skillet and let cool. In the same skillet, heat the remaining 1 tablespoon oil, add the onion, and sauté until translucent, about 5 minutes; remove from the heat and let cool.

In a small bowl, beat together the goat cheese and butter until blended. Add the egg and beat until smooth. Mix in the zucchini, onion, parsley, and cheese.

Using your fingers, loosen the skin from the chicken breasts, leaving one side attached, and force the zucchini stuffing underneath the skin of each breast. Brush each stuffed breast with olive oil and sprinkle lightly with the *herbes de Provence*.

Grill the chicken breasts directly over the heat, turning once, until opaque throughout and the juices no longer run pink, 15 to 20 minutes. If using the oven, place the chicken in a roasting pan and bake for 25 to 30 minutes. Serve at once.

Pumpkin and squash in roasted wedges and creamy mash make
this kaleidoscope of sweet endings—cookies, cake, cheesecake, custard,
ice cream, and pie. They suit a wealth of dining occasions for
many festive interludes.

Desserts

Caramel-Glazed Pumpkin-Date Bars

These bar cookies are quick to mix and bake, and keep especially well. They are perfect with a mug of hot chocolate or cappuccino. MAKES ABOUT 4 DOZEN 1½-INCH SQUARES

½ cup walnuts, pecans, or hazelnuts

½ cup (1 stick) butter

1 cup firmly packed light brown sugar

1 large egg

½ cup pumpkin or winter squash
   purée, canned or homemade

1½ cups all-purpose flour

½ teaspoon baking soda

1 teaspoon ground cinnamon

½ teaspoon ground allspice

½ teaspoon ground ginger

Pinch of salt

¾ cup chopped dates or raisins

CARAMEL GLAZE:

4 tablespoons (½ stick) unsalted
   butter

1 cup confectioners' sugar

½ teaspoon vanilla extract

About 1 tablespoon water

Preheat the oven to 350°F. Lightly butter a 9-by-13-inch baking pan and line the bottom and sides with parchment paper.

Spread the nuts in a small baking pan and bake until lightly toasted, 8 to 10 minutes. If using hazelnuts, rub them between paper towels while they are still warm, letting the papery skins fall off. Chop the nuts coarsely.

In a large bowl, using an electric mixer set on medium speed, beat the butter until creamy. Gradually add the brown sugar, beating until fluffy. Add the egg and pumpkin and beat until smooth. In a medium bowl, stir together the flour, baking soda, cinnamon, allspice, ginger, and salt. Add the dry ingredients to the pumpkin mixture and mix just until incorporated. Stir in the dates and nuts.

Scrape the batter into the prepared pan and smooth the top. Bake until the edges start to pull away from the sides of the pan and a toothpick inserted into the center comes out clean, 18 to 20 minutes. Transfer to a wire rack and let cool for 5 minutes.

Meanwhile, make the Caramel Glaze: In a small saucepan over medium-high heat, melt the butter and cook until it turns a light amber color. Remove from the heat and stir in the confectioners' sugar, vanilla, and enough water to thin to a glaze consistency.

Spread the glaze over the baked bars. Let cool completely. Cut into bars or squares. Store in an airtight container for 3 to 4 days, or wrap tightly and freeze for up to 1 month.

Cranberry-Pecan Pumpkin Drop Cookies

This favorite Halloween spice cookie is perfect for the season. Another time, try this recipe substituting walnuts for the pecans and semisweet chocolate chips for the cranberries for a winning classic. You can use a baking jack-o'-lantern such as a Sugar Pie or canned pumpkin. MAKES 4 DOZEN COOKIES

¾ cup pecan halves

½ cup (1 stick) butter

1 cup firmly packed light brown sugar

1 large egg

⅔ cup pumpkin purée, canned
   or homemade

1 teaspoon vanilla extract

1½ cups all-purpose flour

1 teaspoon baking soda

½ teaspoon baking powder

1 teaspoon ground cinnamon

½ teaspoon ground allspice

½ teaspoon ground cloves

Pinch of salt

1 cup dried cranberries

Preheat the oven to 350°F. Lightly butter 2 baking sheets or line them with parchment paper.

Spread the pecans in a small baking pan and bake until lightly toasted, 8 to 10 minutes. Chop coarsely.

In a large bowl, using an electric mixer set on medium speed, beat the butter until creamy. Gradually add the brown sugar, beating until fluffy. Add the egg, pumpkin, and vanilla and beat until smooth. In a medium bowl, stir together the flour, baking soda, baking powder, cinnamon, allspice, cloves, and salt. Add the dry ingredients to the pumpkin mixture and mix just until incorporated. Stir in the cranberries and pecans.

Drop the batter in rounded teaspoons onto the prepared pans. Bake until golden brown, 12 to 14 minutes. Transfer the cookies to wire racks and let cool. Store in an airtight container for 3 to 4 days, or wrap tightly and freeze for up to 1 month.

Five-Spice Pumpkin-Ginger Cake

✓ EX. ✓

Five-spice powder and the inclusion of two kinds of ginger lend a zingy note to this dark, full-flavored gingerbread with its undertone of pumpkin. This is a variation on a favorite ginger cake I discovered when on a sojourn to Queensland, Australia, where fresh ginger is a prime product. The cake is delectable served warm for dessert, with whipped cream that melts into the warm chocolate chips and crystallized ginger on top. MAKES ONE 9-INCH CAKE; SERVES 12

6 tablespoons (¾ stick) butter, melted

3 tablespoons grated peeled fresh ginger

½ cup honey

½ cup molasses

⅔ cup pumpkin purée, homemade or canned

½ cup plain low-fat yogurt

2 large eggs

2 cups unbleached all-purpose flour

1½ teaspoons baking soda

1 teaspoon Chinese five-spice powder

1 teaspoon ground cinnamon

Pinch of salt

½ cup thinly slivered crystallized ginger

¾ cup semisweet chocolate chips

Whipped cream or ice cream for serving (optional)

very moist

Preheat the oven to 375°F. Lightly butter a 9-inch round baking pan 2 inches deep or a 9-inch springform pan and line the bottom and sides with parchment paper.

In a large bowl, combine the melted butter, fresh ginger, honey, and molasses. Using an electric mixer set on medium speed, beat until well mixed. Add the pumpkin, yogurt, and eggs and beat until smooth. In a medium bowl, stir together the flour, baking soda, five-spice powder, cinnamon, and salt. Add the dry ingredients to the pumpkin mixture and mix just until incorporated.

Scrape the batter into the prepared pan and smooth the top. Sprinkle the top with the crystallized ginger and chocolate chips. Bake until a toothpick inserted into the center comes out clean, 30 to 35 minutes. Transfer to a wire rack and let cool for about 5 minutes. Remove from the pan and peel off the parchment paper. Serve warm or at room temperature, cut into wedges and topped with whipped cream, if desired.

Pineapple-Pumpkin Walnut Cake
with Cream Cheese Frosting

Here is a cake to carry in the pan to a potluck and serve a crowd! Lots of toasted walnuts and coconut lace its moist texture. You can adorn the frosting with a holiday design: Place ¼ cup of semisweet chocolate chips in a small lock-top plastic bag and melt in simmering water. Snip a tiny corner of the bag and pipe a whimsical design on the frosting, like a big jack-o'-lantern face. Bake the cake a day in advance if you wish, as it keeps beautifully. MAKES ONE 9-BY-13-INCH CAKE; SERVES 16

1½ cups walnuts

3 cups unbleached all-purpose flour

1½ cups granulated sugar

1 cup firmly packed light brown sugar

2 teaspoons baking soda

¾ teaspoon salt

1 tablespoon ground cinnamon

½ teaspoon Chinese five-spice powder

1¼ cups canola oil

4 large eggs, lightly beaten

1 tablespoon vanilla extract

1⅓ cups pumpkin purée, canned
   or homemade

¾ cup drained crushed pineapple

1½ cups shredded sweetened
   coconut

CREAM CHEESE FROSTING:

3 ounces cream cheese, at room
   temperature

3 tablespoons unsalted butter, at
   room temperature

1½ cups confectioners' sugar

1 teaspoon vanilla extract

2 to 3 tablespoons milk

Preheat the oven to 350°F. Lightly butter a 9-by-13-inch baking pan and line the bottom and sides with parchment paper.

Spread the walnuts in a small baking pan and bake until lightly toasted, 8 to 10 minutes. Chop coarsely and set aside.

In a large bowl, stir together the flour, granulated sugar, brown sugar, baking soda, salt, cinnamon, and five-spice powder. Add the oil, eggs, and vanilla and, using an electric mixer set on medium speed, beat until smooth. Add the pumpkin and pineapple and mix just until incorporated. Fold in the walnuts and coconut.

Scrape the batter into the prepared pan and smooth the top. Bake until a toothpick inserted into the center comes out clean, 60 to 65 minutes. Transfer to a wire rack and let cool for 10 minutes.

Meanwhile, make the Cream Cheese Frosting: In a medium bowl, using an electric mixer set on medium speed, beat together the cream cheese and butter until creamy. Beat in the confectioners' sugar, vanilla, and enough milk to make a fluffy frosting. Spread over the top of the cooled cake. Store in an airtight container at room temperature for up to 3 days, or wrap tightly and freeze for up to 1 month.

Pumpkin Cheesecake with Gingersnap Crust

This spicy cheesecake, with its tantalizing, hot and sugary ginger topping, may be a new "must" for your Thanksgiving holiday. It is ideal for baking a day or two in advance. Graham cracker crumbs can substitute for the crushed gingersnaps in the crust, if you prefer. MAKES ONE 9-INCH CHEESECAKE; SERVES 12

GINGERSNAP CRUST:

1½ cups crushed gingersnaps

6 tablespoons unsalted butter, melted

3 tablespoons granulated sugar

1 pound natural or regular cream cheese, at room temperature

¾ cup firmly packed light brown sugar

1¼ cups winter squash or pumpkin purée, canned or homemade

3 large eggs

½ cup heavy (whipping) cream

1 teaspoon vanilla extract

1 teaspoon ground cinnamon

½ teaspoon ground ginger

¼ teaspoon ground cloves

⅓ cup chopped crystallized ginger

To make the Gingersnap Crust, preheat the oven to 350°F. In a small bowl, mix together the crushed gingersnaps, melted butter, and granulated sugar. Pat the mixture into the bottom and 1 inch up the sides of a buttered 9-inch springform pan. Bake just until set and lightly darkened, 4 to 5 minutes. Transfer to a wire rack and let cool.

In a large bowl using an electric mixer set on medium speed, beat the cream cheese and brown sugar until creamy. Add the pumpkin and eggs and beat until smooth. Add the cream, vanilla, cinnamon, ginger, and cloves and continue beating until smooth. Pour into the crust-lined pan.

Bake in the 350° oven until just barely set or a knife inserted in the center comes out clean, 40 to 45 minutes. Let cool completely on a wire rack. Refrigerate until well chilled, about 3 hours. To serve, sprinkle the top with the crystallized ginger, remove the pan sides, and cut into wedges.

Pumpkin-Maple Pecan Pie
with Cognac Whipped Cream

This pie is a classic for the holiday season and a star on the Thanksgiving table. Prepare the flaky crust up to 3 days in advance, if you wish. MAKES ONE 9-INCH PIE; SERVES 8

FLAKY PASTRY DOUGH:

1⅓ cups all-purpose flour

¼ teaspoon salt

½ cup (1 stick) plus 1 tablespoon
  cold butter, diced

¼ cup ice water

3 eggs

½ cup firmly packed light brown
  sugar

⅓ cup pure maple syrup

½ teaspoon salt

½ teaspoon ground cinnamon

¼ teaspoon ground allspice

¼ teaspoon ground ginger

1¾ cups pumpkin purée, canned
  or homemade

1½ cups half-and-half or whole milk

To make the Flaky Pastry Dough, in a food processor, combine the flour and salt and pulse briefly to mix. Scatter the butter over the top and pulse just until the mixture forms coarse crumbs about the size of peas. Drizzle the ice water over the flour mixture and pulse just until the dough starts to come together. Remove from bowl and pat into a disk. Wrap and refrigerate for at least 30 minutes or up to 3 days.

Preheat the oven to 425°F. Place the dough disk on a lightly floured work surface and roll out into a 12-inch round. Fold the dough in half and transfer to a 9-inch pie pan. Unfold and line the pan bottom and sides. Fold the overhang under itself and pinch to create an edge. Prick the dough a few times and place in the freezer for 5 minutes. Transfer to the oven and bake just until lightly golden, about 10 minutes. Transfer to a wire rack and let cool completely.

In a large bowl, whisk the eggs until blended. Add the brown sugar, maple syrup, salt, cinnamon, allspice, and ginger and whisk to mix well. Beat in the pumpkin and half-and-half until smooth. Pour into the partially baked pastry shell.

Reduce the temperature to 350°F. Bake until the filling is set and the crust is golden brown, 35 to 40 minutes. Transfer to a wire rack and let cool slightly. (Leave oven on.)

continued >

CARAMELIZED PECANS:

1 tablespoon honey

1 tablespoon sugar

½ teaspoon ground ginger or
 cinnamon

1 tablespoon water

1 cup pecans

COGNAC WHIPPED CREAM:

1 cup heavy (whipping) cream

2 tablespoons confectioners' sugar

2 tablespoons cognac or rum

Meanwhile, prepare the Caramelized Pecans: Line a baking sheet with parchment paper. In a heavy medium saucepan, combine the honey, sugar, ginger, and water and stir to blend. Bring to a boil over medium heat, add the nuts, and boil for 2 minutes, stirring. Turn out onto the prepared baking sheet and spread in a single layer. Bake until golden brown, 8 to 10 minutes. Remove from the oven and let cool. Sprinkle over the baked pie in a wreath pattern or at random.

To make the whipped cream: In a medium bowl, using an electric mixer on medium-high speed, whip the cream until soft peaks form. Beat in the confectioners' sugar and cognac just until combined.

To serve, cut the warm pie into wedges and top with the whipped cream.

Variation: Omit the Caramelized Pecans. Stud the unbaked pumpkin-filled pastry with pecans in a wreath pattern. Bake as directed.

Honey-Rum Pumpkin Ice Cream

Honey and rum impart a seductive taste—as well as helping to keep the texture easy to scoop—to this creamy custard ice cream. Serve this special homemade treat on its own, or use it to dollop on slices of nut cake or a pecan tart. MAKES 1 QUART; SERVES 4 TO 6

2 cups whole milk or half-and-half

3 large egg yolks

⅓ cup sugar

⅓ cup honey

1 cup pumpkin or winter squash
   purée, canned or homemade

1½ teaspoons ground cinnamon

½ teaspoon ground ginger

¼ teaspoon freshly grated nutmeg

1 cup heavy (whipping) cream

¼ cup dark rum

Prepare a large bowl of ice water.

Place the milk in the top of a double boiler and heat over hot water until steaming. In a large bowl, whisk the egg yolks until blended, then add the sugar and honey and whisk until dissolved. Slowly pour some of the hot milk into the yolk mixture and whisk to blend. Return the mixture to the pan and cook over hot water, stirring constantly, until the custard coats the back of the spoon, about 10 minutes.

In a medium metal bowl, combine the pumpkin, cinnamon, ginger, and nutmeg. Stir in the custard. Immediately nestle the bowl in the larger bowl of ice water and stir the custard occasionally until it cools to room temperature. Stir in the cream, cover, and refrigerate until thoroughly chilled, about 4 hours. Freeze in an ice-cream maker according to the manufacturer's directions. When the ice cream is almost ready, spoon in the rum and churn until blended in, about 2 minutes longer. Place in a container, cover, and freeze until firm, about 2 hours.

Rum-Raisin Variation: Place ¾ cup dark or golden raisins in a bowl and pour over ¼ cup rum; microwave on high for 40 seconds or let steep for 15 minutes. Let cool completely if necessary. Churn the ice cream as directed above and when almost finished, add the raisins and soaking rum and churn until fluffy, about 2 minutes longer. Omit adding the additional ¼ cup rum at the end.

Candied Ginger—Pumpkin Crème Brûlée

Guests love to crack through the crunchy sugar topping into the luscious, creamy, spiced custard beneath. It is smart to bake the brûlées well in advance; they need at least 2 hours in the refrigerator to be properly chilled. Then sugar-coat and torch or broil just before serving. SERVES 6

6 egg yolks

⅓ cup firmly packed light brown sugar

1½ cups heavy (whipping) cream

¾ cup pumpkin purée, canned or homemade

2 tablespoons finely chopped crystallized ginger

¾ teaspoon ground cinnamon

3 tablespoons demerara sugar

Preheat the oven to 275°F. In a medium bowl, whisk the egg yolks until lightened in color. Add the brown sugar and whisk until dissolved. Add the cream, pumpkin, ginger, and cinnamon and whisk until well blended.

Place six 6-ounce ovenproof ramekins or soufflé dishes in a large baking pan. Divide the cream mixture among them, filling to within ¼ inch of the top of the ramekins. Pour boiling water into the pan to come halfway up the sides of the ramekins. Bake for 35 to 40 minutes, or until almost set and the center still has a slight jiggle. Remove the pan from the oven and lift the ramekins from the hot water. Let cool briefly; refrigerate for at least 2 hours or up to 1 day to chill thoroughly.

When ready to serve, place the dishes on a baking sheet and sprinkle 1½ teaspoons of the demerara sugar over each one. Use a handheld torch to caramelize the sugar, or, if you don't have a torch, place the pan under a preheated broiler and, watching carefully to prevent burning, broil until the sugar melts and turns a light golden color. Serve immediately.

Pumpkin Flan
with Caramel Whipped Cream and Ice Cream Balls

This impressive dessert is easy to make in advance for a spectacular finale for guests. Or let it grace the holiday table as a switch from the traditional pie. On a trip to Copenhagen, I was introduced by the Danes to the lily gilding of folding the caramel into whipped cream to serve with ice cream balls alongside flan or crème caramel. SERVES 8

⅔ cup granulated sugar

5 large eggs

½ cup firmly packed light brown sugar

2½ cups whole milk or half-and-half

1¼ cups pumpkin, kabocha, or butternut squash purée, homemade or canned

1 teaspoon vanilla extract

2 teaspoons ground cinnamon

1 teaspoon Chinese five-spice powder

Pinch of salt

1 cup heavy (whipping) cream

Vanilla ice cream balls for serving

Preheat the oven to 350°F. Select a 2-quart baking dish such as a soufflé dish or casserole. Place it in the oven to warm slightly as you prepare the caramel.

In a large, heavy-bottomed skillet over medium heat, melt the granulated sugar, shaking the pan without stirring. Reduce the heat to low and cook until the syrup turns a light amber, 7 to 8 minutes. Quickly pour the caramel into the warmed baking dish and tilt to coat the bottom and sides.

In a large bowl, using an electric mixer set on medium-high speed, beat the eggs until blended. Add the brown sugar and beat until dissolved. Add the milk, pumpkin, vanilla, cinnamon, five-spice powder, and salt and beat until smooth. Pour into the caramel-coated dish. Place the dish in a large baking pan and pour boiling water into the pan to come halfway up the sides of the dish. Bake until set and a knife inserted into the center comes out clean, 50 to 55 minutes. Remove the pan from the oven and lift the flan from the hot water. Let cool briefly, then refrigerate for at least 4 hours or up to 1 day to chill thoroughly.

To serve, loosen the custard by running the tip of a knife around the edges. Place a platter on top and quickly invert. Hold in place until the custard releases and the caramel flows out. Reserve about ¼ cup of the caramel for the topping.

In a small bowl, using an electric mixer set on medium-high speed, whip the cream until soft peaks form. Fold in the reserved ¼ cup caramel. Scoop ice cream balls with a small scoop. Serve the flan accompanied with the whipped cream and ice cream balls.

Index